SHEILA P.

CHIKAN EMBROIDERY
The Floral Whitework of India

SHIRE ETHNOGRAPHY

Cover photograph
Detail of back neck motif, kurtha, Lucknow, late nineteenth century.
(Collection of Saleem Arif, London. Photograph: Sue Ormerod)

Drawings by Imogen Paine

Photographs by Sheila Paine unless otherwise stated.

British Library Cataloguing in Publication Data.

Paine, Sheila.
Chikan Embroidery: the floral whitework of India.
(Shire Ethnography, 12)
1. Indian Embroidery.
I. Title.
746.44'0954.
ISBN 0-7478-0009-X.

Dedicated to my husband Leslie, killed in the DC10 crash, Paris, 1974, whose tales first set me on the road to India.

Published by
SHIRE PUBLICATIONS LTD
Cromwell House, Church Street, Princes Risborough,
Aylesbury, Bucks HP17 9AJ, UK.

Series Editor: Bryan Cranstone

ISBN 0 7478 0009 X

First published 1989

Printed in Great Britain by
C. I. Thomas & Sons (Haverfordwest) Ltd,
Press Buildings, Merlins Bridge, Haverfordwest, Dyfed SA61 1XF.

Contents

Acknowledgements

I should especially like to thank Nawab Mir Abdullah of Lucknow for his invaluable help in my contacts over the years with the *chikan* workers, and my daughter Imogen for her drawings. Thanks also to those who kindly allowed me to photograph their embroideries and to the helpful staff of the museums and libraries where I worked.

4

List of illustrations

1
The textile tradition of India

India is still a land of craftsmen, of hand and muscle power. The barrier of a new toll bridge is raised by a man pulling a rope against the counterbalance of a sack of stones; women on the pavements of Calcutta straighten rusty bent nails with a small hammer; workmen in Delhi roofing a new luxury hotel stand on bamboo struts passing tiles up a human ladder; in small towns when school is out children dressed in British-style uniforms cram into bicycle rickshaws to be pedalled home; at stations and roadside stalls the traveller is served tea, not in a plastic cup but in a small handmade earthenware mug to be thrown away. India may have a nuclear programme but mechanisation has made little impact on everyday tasks.

Craft traditions have likewise remained unchanged. In small workshops men beat iron to make knives, cut wood for furniture and leather for shoes, mould molten brass in small furnaces and weave silks, cottons and carpets on handlooms. These manual skills of India have been passed down from generation to generation over thousands of years. One of the greatest is the production of textiles.

The textiles of India were known in Europe from Greek and Roman times. Around 300 BC, when the ancient Greeks called India Eastern Ethiopia and believed it stretched to the edge of the world, the Greek historian Megasthenes travelled to the court of Chandragupta Maurya, emperor of northern India, and mentioned the Indians wearing flowered garments of the finest muslin. The Digest of the Laws of Justinian, Roman ruler of Byzantium in the sixth century AD, lists the duties charged on Indian cotton goods imported into the city. So fine were they that the Romans called them *textili venti*, woven winds.

Whether any were embroidered or whether the flowers on Megasthenes' garments were woven or embroidered, it is not possible to tell, but by the end of the sixteenth century Indian textiles that were embroidered had found their way into the wealthy homes of Europe. The inventory of Hardwick Hall, Derbyshire, drawn up and signed by Bess of Hardwick in 1601, lists several which are still there. From 1600 to 1800 India was the greatest exporter of textiles the world had ever known, surpassing even China.

Textiles are decorated by various techniques, of which embroidery is only one: brocading, printing, painting, ikat, tie-and-dye are others, all used in India. Indian embroidery is both professional and domestic, professional work normally being done by men and made either for a patron, such as a court or a temple, or commercially for local trade or export. Domestic work is almost always done by women and is closely associated with family life and with social custom: dowry pieces for the home, clothing for weddings and for everyday use, animal trappings and the like. Such domestic work is very localised, families generally remaining in one place, with designs handed down through generations.

Chikan embroidery is in a separate category. It is a craft practised only by Muslims and was confined to Dacca and Calcutta in Bengal and to Lucknow. Bengali work was mainly for the European market and no trace of it remains today, neither in

1. Map of India.

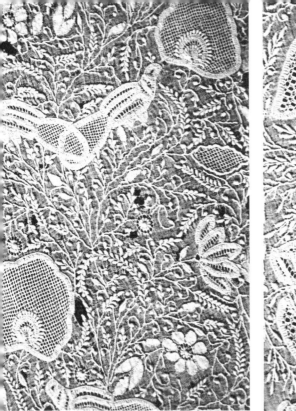

2. (Left) Fragment of *kurtha* bodice; late nineteenth century. The threads of the fine muslin fabric are teased apart and worked into open patterns. Surface stitchery is used to outline these pulled-work areas and to form tiny petals and leaves, creating a complex texture. (Author's collection.)

3. (Right) Fragment of *kurtha* bodice; late nineteenth century. A few large leaves or flowers of pulled work, set in a background of tiny raised petals and leaves linked by trailing stems, are typical of the best *chikan*. (Courtesy of Joss Graham, London.)

Calcutta or in Dacca (now the capital of Bangladesh). In Lucknow embroiderers worked under the patronage of the local courts. When these declined in the mid nineteenth century *chikan* changed from a professional activity of men to a cottage industry for women. It is now almost entirely in the hands of Muslim women and is still a significant industry in Lucknow.

Chikan is a type of whitework, that is to say white embroidery on white fabric, with predominantly floral designs executed on fine cotton with untwisted threads of white cotton, rayon or silk. It is an embroidery that has evolved over centuries, reaching its peak in the late nineteenth century in Lucknow. True *chikan* has the unique property of being limited to a fixed repertoire of stitches, each of which is only ever used in a certain way. This repertoire consists of six basic stitches (five of which are common to other forms of embroidery), five derivatives and seven stitches

4. Dresden cuff. The pulled-work patterns of Dresden are more ornate than _chikan_ and the embroidery has a flatter, lacier quality. (Guildford Museum, G 6782.)

that in themselves form an embossed shape, usually a leaf or petal. These small individual petals help identify _chikan_. In most embroideries the stitchery is balanced by areas of pulled threadwork.

Its discipline gives _chikan_ a pleasing unity but allows for creativity in the choice of combinations of stitches, still within their role of infilling or outlining a design, or creating a shape. It is a discipline shared by no other type of embroidery in the world: European embroiderers, for example, have always used stitches for whatever purpose they pleased.

Another major characteristic of _chikan_, not shared by other whitework, is its great contrast in texture. The embroidery on one piece will range from fine pulled threadwork executed with one thread to heavily embossed stitches worked with as many as twelve. The best work combines the delicacy of one with the chunky quality of the other.

Also distinguishing it from other whitework is the preponderance of trailing stems in the design. These are formed, not with stem stitch as is usually stated, but with a long running stitch, _tepchi_, which allows the thread to be taken to the end of the stem without completely working it. The flower, leaf or pattern at the end is then worked, and the thread is twisted back under the original running stitch, bringing it back to base. This stitch, *tepchi pechni*, is fundamental to all *chikan* and is the essential element of its flowing design.

Though classified as whitework, some of the most beautiful *chikan* of Lucknow (but never that of Bengal) used threads of the wild yellow silk of Assam and Bengal to accentuate pattern in only three stitches of the repertoire.

The background fabric has always been washable: normally fine white cotton, but occasionally thin coloured silk.

Whitework is also a European tradition and *chikan* may be confused with European or hybrid whitework when the articles made are purely western in use. Specifically Indian clothing, for example, has never been embroidered in European whitework techniques.

European whitework is a tradition at least as old as lace and an enduring one. It has progressed through changing styles from the heavy pulled linen of the sixteenth and seventeenth centuries, which was superseded in the eighteenth century by the lace-like work known as Dresden and the tambour hook work introduced from the Orient. In the nineteenth century the finest whitework was the floral embroidery of Ayrshire. The later cutwork of broderie anglaise and Richelieu continued into the early twentieth century. The general introduction of the embroidery machine, invented by Josué Heilmann of Mulhouse in 1828, gradually killed whitework, though it lingered until the mid twentieth century in the pulled linen of peasant clothing and the embroidered trousseaux of continental Europe.

The only types of European whitework that might be difficult to distinguish from *chikan* on, say, infants' robes, handkerchiefs and stoles, are Dresden and Ayrshire. There might also be some confusion with tambour work, originally an oriental technique and often featuring Indian motifs.

Dresden. This pulled embroidery, worked on fine cambric or imported Indian muslin in imitation of lace, was fashionable through the eighteenth century and was made especially in Germany, France, Scandinavia, England and the United States. It was known as Dresden from the capital of Saxony, where much was produced professionally, and as *point de Saxe* or *point de Dresde* in France.

Like *chikan* it combines fine pulled work of varied patterning with motifs in white stitchery. However, in *chikan* usually only two or three pulled-work stitches are combined in the same piece, while the quality of Dresden lies in the juxtaposition of many

5. (Left) Tamboured stole; nineteenth century. Tambour work is strongly linear with only a few small areas of simple openwork. It lacks the textural variety of *chikan*. (Embroiders' Guild collection 2877.)

6. (Right) Ayrshire infant's gown; early nineteenth century. Ayrshire is in some ways closest to *chikan* but openwork areas are cut out of the fabric and filled with needlelace. (Collection of Mrs C. J. J. Turbett, Northamptonshire.)

varied and ornate pulled-work patterns. Whereas the motifs of *chikan* are composed of small flower heads and petals on trailing stems, those of Dresden work are more massed and not necessarily floral but include Renaissance and rococo patterns with tendrils, ribbons and flower baskets of French inspiration. Most embossed stitchery of Dresden is in satin stitch and so lacks the strong textural quality of *chikan*.

Tambour. A tambour hook always produces a simple chain stitch and the embroidery therefore has an essentially linear quality and lacks the variety of stitch and texture of *chikan*. Worked on fine muslin in white cotton, motifs are usually of small floral sprigs and leaves joined by flowing stems, with a few areas of simple pulled work. In addition to the tamboured whitework of Europe, huge quantities were commissioned from Dacca from the seventeenth to the nineteenth centuries and motifs thought suitable for the European market, such as elephants, were commonly chosen. Both Indian and European tambour work are nonetheless easily distinguished from *chikan* by their chain-stitch technique.

Ayrshire. The embroidered muslin of the early nineteenth century for which Ayrshire became particularly famous is more akin to *chikan* in its designs of small flower heads of embossed stitchery and lacy openwork, linked by leaves and trailing stems. It is, however, easily identified by the cut centres of the flowers, worked in a variety of needlelace fillings of immense skill, and the small eyelet holes presaging the later broderie anglaise. True *chikan* never has cut holes, nor does it have needlelace infilling.

Indo-European whitework. Ayrshire was especially popular for infants' robes, many of which were sent or taken out to India by the British in the first half of the nineteenth century. The garment itself, which they were required to copy, its patterns and technique were all alien to Indian *chikan* workers. The result is an inferior product which can easily be distinguished from the original, particularly by the open embroidery. Obliged to cut holes, the Indian embroiderers did not know how to do the needlelace stitches needed to fill them decoratively and resorted to wheels of simple twisted threads. For areas of pulled work they chose the easiest stitch, simple pulled squares known as *jali*, and for the flower petals and leaves made no attempt to use the classic stitches of *chikan* but instead chose mainly satin stitch. Designs

7. Indo-European infant's gown; nineteenth century. Open work areas of copies of Ayrshire made in India are filled with simple *jali* or with crude wheels, while the raised stitchery departs from *chikan* techniques by using stitches such as satin for stems and features European designs such as forked leaves. (Collection of Mrs C. J. J. Turbett, Northamptonshire.)

8. Shift made in India for Emily Hartt, married in Bombay Cathedral in 1883. She had a still-born son in 1884 and died in childbirth in 1885. This simple white embroidery, made to European taste without attempting to copy Ayrshire, is totally unlike *chikan*. It is likely to have been made in Bombay and not in Bengal or Lucknow. (Guildford Museum, NG 1102A.)

9. (Left below) Woman's dress, about 1800-1805, made from white Indian muslin with stripes of open-weave embroidered with a repeat leaf design.

10. (Right below) Detail of the fabric. The embroidery is in the thick stranded cotton used for *chikan*. *Tepchi pechni* is used for the stems and the leaves are of long rough stitches. The pattern has the free-flowing style of Indian embroidery, unlike European, which was normally carefully drawn before being worked. (Courtesy of the Gallery of English Costume, Manchester City Art Galleries, 1922. 1765.)

11. Indo-European infant's gown. Huge areas of pulled work are crudely stitched in *jali*, cut holes are filled with simple wheels and the design is jolly rather than traditional. (Embroiderers' Guild collection, 1825.)

sometimes featured pictorial motifs such as human figures and boats, thought to appeal to the European market.

In addition, as many infants' robes in Ayrshire style were embroidered in India on a square of fabric to be made up in Europe, the embroidery at the front crosses over rather crude seams and the scalloped side edges are joined to form the centre back seam of the robe.

For Indian clothing the best professional work was reserved for the garments of the local rulers, just as the superlative muslins were. In the common oriental tradition such clothes were often made as presentation pieces. Fine long coats (*chogas*), *jama* jackets, front-opening collarless shirts (*kurthas*), fine muslin jackets (*angarkhas*), with a crescent-shaped neckline and cross-over bodice, all were part of the normal dress of the Muslim Mughal princes and of the Hindu Rajas at minor courts. They

12. (Left) *Kurtha* from Lucknow worked mainly in *phunda* with *dohra bakhya* in *muga* silk edged with *zanzeera*. There is *muga* silk braiding at the bodice front and cuffs. (Collection of Saleem Arif, London. Photograph: Alan Tabor.)
13. (Right) Waistcoat worked almost entirely in *khatao* with touches of *mundi murri*. (Courtesy of Joss Graham, London. Photograph: Alan Tabor.)

could be embroidered all over, usually in *tepchi* stitch imitating brocaded weaving, or the edges and corners were all worked in dense *chikan*. Pieces for the narrow crescent yokes of *angarkhas* were often sold separately for garments to be made up by the tailor.

Exquisite work was lavished on small caps. The earliest shape was the *chau goshia*, a four-panel cut, superseded in the mid nineteenth century by five panels meeting at the crown. The rare survivors show some of the finest *chikan* in existence. Later caps were shaped with a flat top like a smoking cap or were made of two sections only, seamed along the top like a glengarry. These were embroidered along the bottom edge, with occasionally an inserted band of embroidery over the crown and flowers over the field. To make them, embroiderers took a square of fine white cotton and worked the double row of *chikan* down the centre, leaving a gap between the rows deep enough to be cut to form the bottom hem when the tailor made up the cap.

Ladies' *saris* are traditionally embroidered with scattered motifs over such fabric as remains to be wound round the body after the front pleating has been done. Denser embroidery forms a band round the hem and covers the *pallava*, the loose part of the *sari*, which then drops from the shoulder. As with piece goods, the more repetitive work required to cover such a long piece of cloth was often the task of women.

Saris are still made for the Indian market, but today most *chikan* is on table linen and on *kurthas* for men and women exported all over the world. There has been a rapid deterioration in the quality of the embroidery: thin coloured silks and synthetics have ousted white muslin, and scrappy white stitches have replaced the textural range of historical *chikan*.

14. *Angarkha* neck pieces; early twentieth century. These 'mass-produced' embroideries were cut and applied to the front neck of the *angarkha*. This example has some stitchery in yellow silk. (Author's collection. Photograph: R. Simpson.)

2
Derivation of the name

The Indian name for *chikan* embroidery is *chikankari, kari* being Hindi for 'work'. The word *chikan* is Persian. Persian was the court language of India, introduced by the Mughals, who came from Central Asia and ruled northern India from 1530 until their empire declined in the mid eighteenth century with the growing power of the British. Persian names were commonly used in their courts, even provincial ones.

Dehkhoda's Persian dictionary, compiled in the 1950s and 1960s, quotes the definition of *chikan* given in earlier dictionaries. The oldest of these is Burhan's classical dictionary of 1651, which describes it as 'a kind of embroidery with gold thread. Quilting'. Later dictionaries give 'embroidery with gold thread', 'embroidery in various kinds of silk on garments and other items'. There is no mention of white, nor of cotton, nor of flowers. The usual Persian word for 'embroidery' is *naksh*, familiar in Europe from the embroidered trouser legs of Persian costume marketed under this name in Europe in the 1840s when Persian women began to adopt western-style dress and sold their old costumes.

Two poets are quoted by Dehkhoda: Radi al-Din Nishaburi, writing in the twelfth century and Kamal al-Din Ismail, writing in the thirteenth. Both use the word *chikan* as a metaphor for 'needle'. 'Needle' is commonly *sozan* in Persian, from which *suzani*, the embroidered hangings and bedspreads of the Uzbeks of Central Asia, is derived.

The first appearance of the word *chikan* in India is in John Richardson's Persian/English dictionary published in Calcutta in 1806. This defines *chikan* or *chikin* as 'a kind of cloth worked with the needle in flowers'. (The word does not appear in his first edition, published in 1777.) The 1852 Steingass revision of Richardson, combined with Johnson's Persian/Arabic/English dictionary, adds 'and gold' to this definition.

Modern Hindi dictionaries give 'embroidered fine muslin' as the meaning of *chikan*. The word is used in the province of Orissa in eastern India to mean chain stitch. This is the stitch normally used to outline appliquéd motifs on the ceremonial umbrellas and banners of that region. It is always in white.

A related term is *chikandoz*, which in Peshawar means colourless embroidery. Here, and in Quetta and Bhopal, the technique is simple quilting and back stitch and is not now considered *chikan* work, though quilting was included in the definition of 1651. *Chikandoz* was also the name given in the nineteenth century to some embroiderers of north-west India, notably the silk workers of Surat and some towns of Sind.

The only Persian word with an associated sound from which *chikan* may derive is *chick* or *chiq*, defined by Yule's glossary of colloquial Anglo-Indian as a 'bamboo screen blind'. John Fryer used this word on his voyage of 1672-81 when describing the women of Bombay: 'The Coach where the Women were, was covered with Cheeks, a sort of hanging Curtain, made with Bents variously coloured with Lacker, and Chequered with Packthred so artificially, that you may see all without, and yourself within unperceived.' There is a strong affinity in the patterns of *chikan* embroidery and those of the window screens that protect Muslim women from public gaze. The Hindi name for these decorated screens, *jali*, is given to the pulled-thread stitches of *chikan*.

Derivation from a place-name, either in India, as *chikan* is an Indian embroidery, or in Persia, has sometimes been suggested. Gazetteers of India list no village or town sounding remotely like chikan. In north-western Iran there is a village in the Ramand administration near Qazvin called Chikin. The occupations of the inhabitants are agriculture and the weaving of kilims and garments of goats' hair. In Ancient Persia the only place with a name resembling *chikan* was Circan, a region south-west of Kabul, west of Gujarat, north of Sind, 29°N and 109°W. John Speede's map of the Kingdom of Persia dated 1626 describes this area as 'Gedrolia now Circan, neare the Mare Indicum, a barren Countrey, scarce worth a farther description.'

15. The ornately carved wooden window screens of Mughal buildings bear the same name (*jali*) as the pulled-work patterns of *chikan*. Jodhpur, Rajasthan.

3
History

The present Begum of Rampur, recalling her erstwhile fairytale wealth, mentions that the beautiful *chikan* embroideries she owned were so fragile that they survived only three washes and were then thrown away.

Though examples of other Indian embroideries remain from the seventeenth century, of the washable household linen and everyday white clothing of *chikan* the earliest survivors are a few nineteenth-century pieces. With no early examples extant, pinpointing the exact date of the emergence of *chikan* is virtually impossible. However, the various types of flowered muslins from which it certainly derived are recorded in documents and in paintings from the seventeenth century. Developing from these early flowered muslins, with the additional influence of eighteenth-century European whitework, *chikan* crystallised into its definitive form in the nineteenth century. The story of this development can be traced from such sources as paintings, travellers' accounts and trade records.

Trade with Europe

Trade between Europe and India existed long before the Portuguese, nudging their way down the West African coast with the help of newly invented navigational instruments, rounded the Cape of Good Hope in 1487, and in 1498, with Vasco da Gama, reached India. The route before the discovery of the Cape had been via the Red Sea or the Persian Gulf. T. Mun, a deputy of the East India Company writing in about 1620, recorded that from there, 'the Merchandise (with great charges) were often transported overland by the Turkes, upon cammels, fiftie dayes journey, unto Aleppo in Soria and to Alexandria in Egypt.'

The new maritime routes were exploited by the Portuguese, English, Dutch and French. Each nation established mercantile ports and East India trading companies to control a three-stage commerce between Europe, India and south-east Asia in bullion, textiles and spices. Bullion, loaded on ships in Europe, was exchanged for cotton piece goods in India, which were then bartered for spices in the Malay archipelago.

With the establishment of regular commercial contacts in the sixteenth century, records become available, in the form both of travellers' stories and of trading accounts of the East India companies. Though trade in flowered muslins is recorded this may refer to fabrics worked in gold or silk rather than white cotton, or brocaded rather than embroidered. No specific reference to fine white fabrics embroidered with a needle in white cotton thread in floral patterning that includes pulled work has been found.

Accounts of the early merchants and travellers are variable in their accuracy. Some detail only the horrors of the voyage, others record meticulously all they saw. Bernier, for example, a doctor from Montpellier University visiting the estates of the Great Moghul in the late sixteenth century, describes the ladies' drawers which have become legendary: 'so fine and delicate that in certain circumstances they last only one night, even though they are often worth ten or twelve crowns and sometimes more when they are the kind I have seen, enriched with fine needle embroidery'.

Linschoten, a Dutchman travelling to India in 1585, states clearly that the decoration he saw was weaving and not embroidery. The women's dress was 'so fine that you may see all their body through it . . . these clothes are very faire, some of them being very costly wroughte with Loom-worke, and divers figures and flowers of all colours.'

The 'Loom-worke' decorating muslins was *jamdani* weaving, a very fine brocading technique practised only in Dacca, though after 1850 it was also produced in Taandah near Faizabad to the east of Lucknow. It is still made in Dacca. Normally two men work together at the same loom, one at each side. As weaving progresses they insert at regular intervals a geometric motif or flower in white or coloured cotton or silk, or in gold or silver wire. *Jamdani* weaving is one of the sources of *chikan*, the decoration in *tepchi* stitches of piece goods being a simpler version of the more skilled weaving. Following the weft and warp threads, the floral patterns of *jamdani* were of necessity more stylised than *chikan* designs. Requiring no loom, embroidery was often a cheaper copy of a woven decoration, as in the embroidered shawls of Kashmir.

By the mid seventeenth century a direct commerce in Indian textiles for the European market had been established. The most successful trade was in the painted and resist-dyed cottons known as 'chintzes', but embroideries were also exported. They came from two distinct regions: Gujarat in the north-west and Bengal in the north-east. The sixteenth- and seventeenth-century embroideries of Gujarat were bedspreads and hangings with flowing branches, flowers and birds worked in multicoloured chain stitch on cotton. They have no connection with *chikan*. Those of Bengal were the Indo-Portuguese bedspreads depicting biblical or Indian stories, worked in chain and back stitch in the local wild yellow silks on white cotton.

Also traded in quantity from Bengal were fine white muslins. Almost without exception every European merchant in India in the seventeenth century comments on the incredibly fine cottons, the sheerest of which were those of Bengal, mainly made around Dacca.

Bengal is a low-lying tropical region of deltaic silt, laced by wide rivers, innumerable small waterways and stagnant pools. The climate of the Dacca area in particular favoured the cultivation of a type of cotton that could be spun very finely and the high humidity prevented the delicate threads breaking on contact with air. The spinners could work only during the rainy season and often spun the thread over steam from boiling water to raise the humidity still further. As the Ganges and Brahmaputra rivers had properties particularly suitable for bleaching, the cottons were not only fine but very white.

Records of the mercantile companies give a factual account of the textiles traded from Bengal. Orders for the year 1681, for example, included '500 *mulmuls* with fine needleworke flowers wrought with white, the flowers to be about three or four inches asunder and neat.' Though referred to as needlework, the spacing of the flowers indicates that this could perhaps be *jamdani* weaving. It is, however, clear that fine white cottons with repeat motifs of isolated flowers worked in white thread were one of the textiles exported to Europe from Bengal.

They were also marketed around the towns and villages of England. Writing on 'The Great Reclothing of Rural England', Margaret Spufford quotes the *Plain Dealing Linnen Draper* published in 1696: 'the lighter dimities, sometimes flowered white, and cotton dimities, and cotton diapers from the East Indies were used for men's and women's waistcoats and for women's petticoats.' Clearly the itinerant pedlars already had flowered Indian cottons among their wares.

It was not until the eighteenth century that a cotton industry developed in Europe. The white fabric of Europe was linen and even the 'Manchester cottons' of the mid seventeenth century were actually wool. Only by the 1780s were the quantities produced sufficient to meet demand and until then cotton continued to be imported from India.

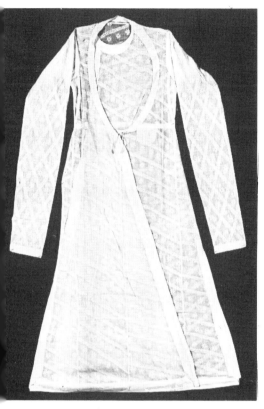
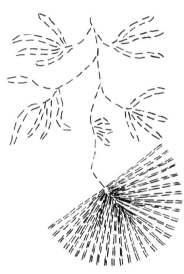

16. (Left) *Angarkha* in white muslin with *tepchi* work, strongly imitative of *jamdani* weaving. (Calico Museum of Textiles, Ahmedabad.)
17. (Right) Carnation sprig on fabric swatch from Barbara Johnson's album, 1768. (By courtesy of the Trustees of the Victoria and Albert Museum.)

Severe measures were taken to protect the infant cotton industry of Europe and heavy customs duties were imposed. In 1787 18 per cent was levied on 'white calicoes flowered or stitched' imported into England by the East India Company. It is in eighteenth-century trade records that a distinction is made between 'flowered' and 'stitched'.

In 1793 the East India Company listed the muslins imported and sold two years previously by the French Compagnie des Indes at Lorient. From a total of £127,788 worth of muslin varieties described as flowered, £861 of one fabric, *momoodie*, specifically described as 'stitched', was sold. The highest-priced plain muslins fetched 100 shillings a piece, the stitched *momoodies* 26 shillings and the flowered muslins between 33 and 50 shillings. The conclusion could be drawn that the flowered muslins were woven and not stitched, as embroidery was so often a cheaper version of the more skilful weaving. It is reasonable to presume that the stitched *momoodies* were floral.

Support for this assumption can be found in an album now in the Victoria and Albert Museum, London. This was devised by Barbara Johnson, daughter of a Buckinghamshire cleric, who lived from 1746 to 1823 and through most of her life saved swatches of the fabrics she bought or was given for her dresses, putting them in her album and recording their price, length, name and the date. Among them is a small piece of fine white cotton she paid 10 shillings a yard for in 1768, a very high price for that time. It is flowered with a sprig of one carnation head and leaves and is embroidered with one of the stitches of *chikan, tepchi*. It is quite a large motif, but was probably repeated over the fabric. This swatch seems to be the earliest known dated piece of exported white Indian embroidery in a *chikan* stitch.

It was in the eighteenth century that England's relationship with India changed from that of a trading partner to an imperial power. After Clive's victory at Plassey in 1757 the British settled their newly won empire. At first a handful of British officials and soldiers controlled the territory, a few accompanied by their wives. In Bombay it had been the custom of the East India Company to send out 'a supply of women to their possessions in the East. They were classed as 'gentle women' and 'other women'.' But it was in Calcutta that most Englishwomen settled, though their number remained small. A list published in Calcutta in 1902 of the 'Europeans and Others in the English Factories in Bengal at the time of the siege of Calcutta in the year 1756' names 593 men and 145 women. There was an influx of officers between 1778 and 1785 but Englishmen still 'were seldom able to find any but Indian or half-caste mistresses in Calcutta.' From this period on it became customary for wives and more particularly husband-seekers to come out to India.

These women would certainly have brought whitework embroideries among their personal belongings, whereas earlier traders from Britain had brought only woollen goods to sell. By 1813 it was customary for European women to retain an Indian tailor in their household and they would have commissioned from local artisans copies of their embroideries as well as their clothing.

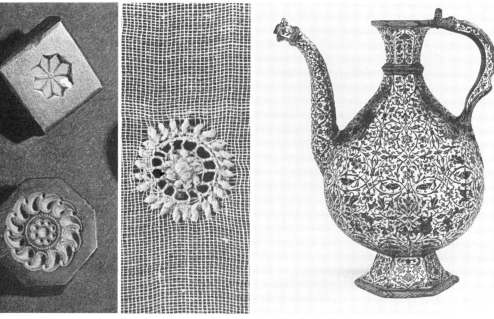

18. (Left) Jeweller's moulds with floral motifs, and a flower in a combination stitch of *chikan* featuring the stitch *banarsi* around the edge. (Photograph of moulds: R. Simpson.)
19. (Right) The inlaid pattern of silver and brass on this seventeenth-century ewer from the Deccan has the same flower heads linked by curving stems and small leaves as is typical of *chikan*. (By courtesy of the Trustees of the Victoria and Albert Museum, 1479-1904.)

This period of the end of the eighteenth century marks the beginning of *chikan* proper. The stitched *momoodies*, Barbara Johnson's dress fabric and the earlier flowered muslins, even when embroidered and not woven, were sprigged. Flowers and leaves were not linked by trailing stems and, most important of all, there were no leaf designs of pulled work. This element the Indian artisan absorbed from the European whitework of the late eighteenth century — Dresden work — and incorporated into the white floral embroidery that belonged to India's Mughal heritage.

The Mughal heritage
The great Islamic empires of the sixteenth and seventeenth centuries were those of Safavid Persia, Mughal India and Ottoman Turkey. All were wealthy and in all the decorative arts thrived.

As the Mughal rulers set up their courts in India they organised

20. Courtier watching the return of Shah Jahan to his father Jahangir about 1645, from the Padshahnama of Abd al-Hamid Lahori. The floral border of his coat is worked in white and not the more usual gold. (Reproduced by gracious permission of Her Majesty the Queen.)

royal workshops based on the Persian *karkhanas*. Here artisans produced paintings, textiles, jewels, arms and artefacts in metal, stone, wood, mother-of-pearl and enamel. Their decorative arts, indeed even buildings (such as the Taj Mahal), share a common design tradition of floral inspiration.

Under Mughal rule the slightly stiff Persian repeat patterns of flower heads, often set in diapers or rows, gradually developed into a local Indian style that was more flowing. The inspiration for these floral patterns is accepted as being the Persian love and symbolism of the garden, fuelled by the Mughal ruler Jahangir's delight at the flowers he saw on his visit to Kashmir in 1620, and the European herbals which found their way to the Mughal courts, in the seventeenth century. The floral designs of *chikan* share the same heritage.

The work of weavers and embroiderers can be seen in the contemporary miniature paintings of the Mughal courts where details are recorded with meticulous precision. Seated on floral carpets under embroidered canopies, holding court, talking with scholars, taking refreshment, the Mughal rulers and courtiers are usually depicted wearing transparent coats decorated with a repeating motif of isolated flowers in white, silk or gold. This is most probably *jamdani* weaving but it is impossible to be sure. When the edges of the garment are worked with a more flowing floral design it is usually in gold. Far more rarely it is in whitework, as is the coat of a courtier in a painting prepared for the Mughal ruler Shah Jahan in about 1645. The border of cursive floral pattern appears to be in flat white stitchery, certainly a precursor of *chikan.*

Persia

Persian was the normal court language of the Mughals and the name *chikan* with its Persian origin undoubtedly came to India with them. Whether an actual technique of whitework embroidery did too is problematical. The twelfth- and thirteenth-century use in Persian poetry of the word as a metaphor for needle may allude to the visible needle pricks characteristic of quilting. Relevance to the embroidery now known as *chikan* cannot necessarily be assumed.

Carpets and brocades were the most renowned textile products of the Persians, though Marco Polo commented that they made 'wonderful things in silke and Embroyderie'. While the seventeenth-century travellers to Bengal were marvelling at the fine cottons they saw there, those to Persia were commenting mainly on the silks embroidered with flowers in gold and coloured silk, and on the painted cotton cloths. The French chevalier Chardin, who went to Persia in 1671, noticed that the bazaars were full of Indian goods and that Bengali cotton was imported as it was finer and cheaper than the Persian variety.

Whitework was indeed also made in Persia, in the technique known as *filo tirato.* This means that the threads are drawn out of the fabric rather than teased apart as in *chikan.* Removing threads in this manner automatically gives straight lines rather than curves. Patterns therefore tend to be geometric and not floral and surviving Persian whitework of the nineteenth century is of crosses, squares and diagonals filled with intricate detailing. It is not like *chikan.*

Bengal

There is no concrete evidence for the usual claim that *chikan* began in Bengal and then moved to Lucknow, though the situation in Bengal in the late eighteenth century lends weight to such a supposition. There was more extensive European settlement and trade there than elsewhere in India and a centuries-old tradition of textile skills, whereas at the same period the rulers of Oudh, the Muslim Nawabs, were just establishing their capital at Lucknow and attracting master artisans into their service. However, the *chikan* work of Bengal and Lucknow was significantly different; in Bengal it was principally piece goods for trade that were made, with some patronage of small local rulers, and in Lucknow clothing for wealthy royal courts.

James Taylor, an English surgeon reporting on the topography and statistics of Dacca in 1840, remarked that embroidery in Dacca was in the hands of three distinct groups of Muslims. One was the *ruffogurs* (or *rafogars),* highly skilled darners whose job was to pull out faulty threads in the muslins and *jamdanis* and replace them using a needle. Taylor claimed that the *rafogars* were all 'opium eaters' and worked well only under its influence. These workers are categorised as embroiderers because they used needles. The other groups were the *zurdose,* who embroidered muslin with silk, gold and silver, and the *chuckendose,* who were responsible for the 'flowering of muslin dresses'. This flowering must have been embroidery in white cotton threads, as silk and metal threads on muslin came into the category of *zurdose* work. The embroidery in *muga* thread of *khaseidas,* the best known embroideries of Dacca, which were turban lengths exported in quantity to the Middle East, was the task of low-class Muslim women and thus placed in a separate category by Taylor.

The flowered muslins were sent to other parts of India and were an important export for Dacca, though between 1817 and 1834 the volume of cotton goods exported fell by three-quarters, the monopoly of the East India Company ending in 1833 and exposing the Indian weaver to the full blast of the competition from English cotton of the Industrial Revolution. Most of the weavers of Dacca abandoned their looms and the population fell from 200,000 in 1800 to 68,000 in 1838. It was in 1817 that the commercial residency was abolished and the export of cloth to Europe ceased. Possibly at this period workers moved to

21. (Right) Sample of *chikan* made in Dacca from John Forbes Watson's collection of specimens and illustrations of the textile manufactures of India, 1873-80. Both stitchery and pattern closely imitate *jamdani* weaving. (By courtesy of the Trustees of the Victoria and Albert Museum, London.)

22. (Below) Handkerchief made in Calcutta; mid nineteenth century. This fine piece is worked with many of the traditional *chikan* stitches but in a naive design featuring figures like those on the infant's robe (figure 11) and an engagingly childlike rendering of steam engines. (By courtesy of the trustees of the Victoria and Albert Museum, IS 0542.)

Lucknow, where the court gave them patronage.

Harriet Tytler, an Englishwoman who stayed in Dacca in 1852, reports that the gauze-like muslin for which Dacca was famous 'used to sell for £1 10s a yard and had to be made under ground for so fine was its texture that the slightest breath of air would have destroyed it while being woven', but that by the time she there 'they made no more of this lovely quality as there was no market for it. The best then made was sold at 2s 8d a yard. The reason there was no market for it was the nawabs and rajahs began to wear English clothes and went up to the Hills in the hot weather. There were only two old men then alive who in their younger days used to make the beautiful kind.' She comments on Dacca's embroideries in silver and gold, as well as silks, but makes no mention of *chikan*.

Dr John Forbes Watson, reporting on Indian fabrics to the Secretary of State for India in Council, includes in his pattern books of 1867 some examples of *chikan*. These come only from Dacca and are grouped with *jamdanis,* striped and plain muslins. The *chikan* embroidery patterns are strongly imitative of *jamdani* weaving, that is to say that the pattern follows diagonal lines or diapers and is on piece goods. Floral sprigs are worked mainly in satin stitch in heavy white cotton thread, and pulled work is restricted to small areas and simple technique.

Calcutta was the great trading port of Bengal and capital of the British Raj. The cloth merchants of Dacca would take their muslins there in November both for local sale and to load on Arab ships returning with the monsoon. There is some confusion over what *chikan* was made in Calcutta and what traded there from Dacca, but by the mid nineteenth century intricately worked handkerchiefs which have little in common with the piece goods of Dacca were attributed to Calcutta. They show a strong European influence both in technique and in the use of pictorial motifs thought suitable for English taste.

One especially fine example was shown at the Paris Exhibition of 1867 and it is certain that the trade exhibitions of the nineteenth century fostered outstanding work. At the Calcutta International Exhibition of 1883-4 only a few pieces of *chikan* were shown from Calcutta, mainly handkerchiefs, which won no prizes, whereas a great variety of prizewinning work was submitted from Lucknow.

A report on the art manufactures of India in 1888 by T. N. Mukharji records that 'in Calcutta large quantities of cotton embroidery, called *chikan,* are sold among Europeans. Hand-

23. Portrait of the Nawab Asab ud-Daula wearing the feathered crown of the Nawabs and a coat with white decoration that could be *jamdani* or *chikan*. (State Museum, Lucknow.)

kerchiefs, ladies' dresses, and clothing for children are also embroidered by men residing in the neighbouring Districts.' Mukharji praises the *jamdanis* of Dacca but makes only passing reference to embroidery there: 'embroidery with cotton thread is known by the general name of *chikan-dozi.*' He then describes the importance of *chikan* in Lucknow.

In 1905 the *Indian Almanac*, listing all the trades and professions of Calcutta down to dancing teachers and billiard-table manufacturers, makes no mention of embroiderers. Neither does the Gazetteer of 1908, though it does mention a few embroiderers in nearby Hooghly.

Lucknow

The resplendent eighteenth-century court of Oudh shifted between Faizabad and Lucknow, attracting scholars, jewellers,

24. (Left) Detail of canopy from the painting 'Chess Game in the Zenana', about 1780. The floral style of this canopy is not related to the stitchery of *chikan* and it appears to be worked in flat surface embroidery. (By courtesy of Sotheby's.)
25. (Right) Feathered crown worked in *jamdani* over the surface of a *kurtha*, undoubtedly made for the Nawab. The edges of the garment are bordered with *chikan*. (State Museum, Lucknow, 52.71.1.)

metalworkers, embroiderers and other craftsmen from the declining courts of Delhi and Murshidabad. The rich and powerful Nawab Shuja-ud-Daula employed European officers to reorganise his armies, British artists to paint his family and local artisans to embroider, enamel and encrust with jewels magnificent ceremonial artefacts: *huqqas* for smoking tobacco through water and *pan* sets for chewing spices. On his death in 1775 his successor, Asaf-ud-Daula, moved the court to Lucknow and pitched his tastes to ever greater opulence, presiding eventually over a toy-town charade of caparisoned elephants, nightly fireworks and regal banquets in chandeliered palaces. More artisans flocked to his luxury-loving court and Sir George Watt, writing on the Indian arts in 1903, suggests that it was at this period of the late eighteenth century that *chikan* embroidery began in Lucknow, though it was for gold and silver embroidery that Lucknow was then renowned throughout India.

The many miniature paintings of the School of Oudh and Lucknow of 1760 to 1775, and those of the School of Murshidabad, show the same garments of transparent cotton with all-over repeating floral motifs as the earlier Mughal paintings, though a European-inspired painting of the women of the court of Oudh in about 1780 shows a canopy and dais cover of white flowers that is clearly embroidery, but without the characteristics of *chikan*.

The decline of the courts through the early nineteenth century and the Mutiny of 1857 reduced Lucknow to poverty and distress, from which it only gradually recovered as trade was boosted by the railways, built by the British after the Mutiny taught them the importance of easy communications in ruling their Indian empire.

In this commercial setting *chikan* embroidery revived and trade replaced patronage.

William Hoey, sent to Lucknow in 1880 to assess how much tax the British government could extract from each category of Indian worker, remarks that *chikan* had flourished there for the previous twenty years but was virtually unknown in the time of the Nawabs. As a tax inspector, presumably a practical man not given to flights of fancy, his statements have particular validity. Nonetheless, that *chikan* of very high quality was produced in the Nawabi period is proved by two pieces now in the State Museum of Lucknow. These are a *kurtha* in fine *jamdani* patterned with the feathered crown of the Nawabs of Oudh and bordered with *chikan*, and a *jamdani angarkha* with the name of the man who presented it to his ruler worked in *chikan* in Persian script around the hem.

Hoey comments on how much the industry had grown since the Mutiny in 1857 and how by the 1880s about 1200 women and children, who had 'seen better days' before being impoverished by the final abolition of the court, were working as *chikan* embroiderers. It was by this period that Lucknow had refined *chikan* into an individual embroidery style.

The nineteenth-century exhibitions, launched by the Great Exhibition of 1851, must have acted as an impetus to perfecting technique. Though Lucknow exhibited no *chikan* at the Agra exhibition of 1867, its workshops were major prizewinners at the Calcutta International Exhibition of 1883-4 and the Indian and Colonial Exhibition of 1886.

In the 1880s *chikan* from Lucknow was exported to Calcutta, where local manufacture had virtually died. By 1904 it was one of the most important industries of Lucknow and was in the hands of a few firms. One, established in 1890 and still active today, offered in 1901 over one thousand different designs of *chikan*.

4
Technique

Holding the background fabric under tension is a prerequisite of all embroidery techniques. This is normally achieved by stretching it over a frame.

In the case of *chikan* embroidery no frame is used. The fabric is stretched taut around the index finger and wedged between the other fingers to hold it in position. The little finger is swung across the palm to restrain the fabric still further. The thumb is free and used to control the progress of the needle. The suppleness of hand these movements demand results from generations of working *chikan* embroidery and is impossible for most people to emulate.

The caste system of India, whereby the son of an embroiderer automatically becomes an embroiderer, has ensured such hereditary dexterity through thousands of years. The *chikan* workers are Muslim, outside the Hindu caste system, but they have the same tradition of families always following a single profession. Learning at an early age imparts, as in language skills, an inbuilt physical facility to cope with esoteric demands. Young trainees brought in to revive *chikan* are unable to execute these movements and use a small circular frame.

Past writers on whitework have all stressed that in *chikan* the embroiderer pulls the thread away from the body, rather than towards it, as in Europe. This is not strictly true: it is simply that the method of holding the fabric taut automatically means that the thread is pulled upward, but not necessarily in a forward or backward direction.

Another peculiarity of *chikan* is that some stitches are always worked from the back of the fabric and others from the front. In contrast to much European whitework, no holes are ever cut in the fabric and threads are not normally drawn, but only teased apart.

5
Materials

Fabrics

The traditional fabrics of *chikan* were fine white cottons. In Bengal these were produced on the handlooms of Dacca. In Lucknow the area of the town known as Madmudnagar was the quarter of the weavers until the early twentieth century. The muslin (*malmal*), cambric (*adhi*) and glazed cambric (*tanzeb*) produced here were preferred for *chikan* work to the imported European cottons. All cottons are now commercially produced in Indian mills. In modern times thin coloured Jap silk and cotton/polyester mixtures have also been used, changing the character of *chikan*.

Needles

A thick crewel needle 3.5 cm (1⅓ inches) long with a small eye is used for embroidery, and one 5.5 cm (2⅕ inches) long for pulled work. Formerly imported from Europe, they are now made in India.

Threads

Very fine stranded white cotton, bleached or unbleached and of Indian origin, is used for embroidery. This thread is delivered to the embroiderer in large hanks by a Hindu trader. To separate a hank of untwisted thread into the requisite number of strands for working, the embroiderer sits and winds it round the big toe of the right foot. Pulling the thread towards her, she separates the large hank into smaller ones of six strands. This number is chosen because, though some *chikan* stitches are traditionally worked with one strand and others with twelve or fourteen, the majority are with six.

For pulled work a thread is usually drawn from the selvedge of the fabric, as it is stronger.

Today the fashion is for two coloured threads to be used together, giving a shaded effect.

A few special pieces of the nineteenth century have pink thread quilted into the design, usually outlining the motifs or accentuating seams.

Chikan of the late nineteenth and early twentieth century was occasionally worked in gold plate thread. This clumsy technique limited the range of stitches and designs to such an extent that it can hardly be considered *chikan*, though it was marketed as such.

Muga silk

A feature of some of the most beautiful work of Lucknow, but surprisingly not that of Dacca and Calcutta, is the use of yellow silk as a contrast. Only three of the stitches of *chikan* are ever highlighted in this way.

Yellow silk grows wild in Bengal and Assam and is of three varieties: *tasar, eri* and *muga*. The one highlighting the embroidery of Lucknow is *muga* (*Antheraea assama*). It is indigenous to Assam and cultivated by the tribal people of that region and in Bengal. It is a rich golden colour.

This wild yellow silk was a source of amazement to the seventeenth-century travellers, who mistook it for a grass, as the cocoon hangs on a plant or tree and so appears to be part of it. It was also traded from Bengal: with the rice and fine white cloth he observed being shipped from the port of Orissa, the merchant seaman Master Caesar Frederike lists also 'great store of cloth of Herbes, which is a kind of silke' and describes how it 'groweth amongst the woods without any labour of man, and when the bole thereof is growne round as bigge as an Orange, then they take care onely to gether them.'

The Portuguese called the silk *Herba de Bengala* and it became familiar in Europe through the Indo-Portuguese quilts and bedhangings of the sixteenth and early seventeenth centuries. Its use in *chikan* died out in the early years of the twentieth century.

6
Stitches

Chikan embroiderers claim a repertoire of about forty stitches, to which they give delightfully fanciful names: double-star ear-ring, cowrie shell, peacock feather's eye. Closer analysis reveals that many of these are different combinations of the same few basic stitches.

The first major division is between the embroidery stitches themselves and the pulled threadwork; indeed, the two are traditionally done by different workers. Within the range of embroidery stitches it is important to distinguish between the simple basic stitches and their derivatives, and the stitches which in themselves form a shape. Finally, combinations of stitches, which in theory are limitless, form the group that gives the skilled worker scope for creativity.

Chikan embroidery is unique in its discipline: each stitch is used for one purpose only. Chain stitch, for example, will never be used to work a stem or a small leaf or flower, but only the final outline of a large leaf or petal, nor will the number of threads used to work it vary — it is always worked with one only. No other embroidery in the world shares this characteristic.

Basic stitches

The basic stitches are six in number and all except one are common to other forms of embroidery. They are *tepchi* (running stitch), *bakhya* (double back or shadow stitch), *hool* (detached eyelet), *zanzeera* (chain stitch), *rahet* (stem stitch) and *banarsi*, which has no European equivalent.

The introduction of any other basic stitches outside this repertoire indicates that the work is not true *chikan*. Indo-European whitework of the nineteenth century, for example, adds feather stitch on seams, flowers of satin stitch and cut broderie anglaise.

Tepchi is a long running stitch worked with six strands on the right side of the fabric taken over four threads and picking up one, so that a line is formed. It is used principally as a basis for further stitchery and occasionally to form a simple shape.

Tepchi was considered the cheapest and quickest of the *chikan* stitches and piece goods, such as some exported to Europe in the eighteenth century, were sometimes executed entirely in it. It closely resembles *jamdani* weaving in appearance.

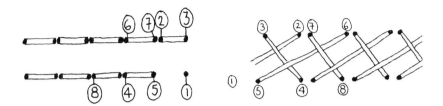

26. *Bakhya*, showing the front (left) and the back (right).

Bakhya is a close herringbone worked from left to right with six strands on the wrong side of the fabric. When close herringbone is worked from the reverse of the fabric it forms a line of back stitches on the front and is known in western embroidery as double back stitch. In *chikan* it is used for shadow work of petals and leaves.

Bakhya exploits the fineness of the background fabric and in some *chikan* this stitch is used alone to work all the flowers. Most modern degraded work is a rough attempt at *bakhya*.

Hool is a fine detached eyelet stitch. A hole is punched in the fabric with the needle and the threads are teased apart. The hole is then held by small straight stitches all round, worked with one thread on the right side of the fabric. In combination stitches it can be worked with six threads and often forms the centre of a flower.

Zanzeera is a small chain stitch worked with one thread on the right side of the fabric. The thread is looped around the needle, which picks up about two threads of fabric, and the needle is then reinserted in the previous loop, forming a chain. *Zanzeera* is extremely fine and is used as a final outline to leaf or petal shapes after one or more outlines have already been worked. These are normally in *dohra bakhya, balda* and *banarsi.*

Zanzeera can very occasionally be in yellow *muga* silk and is one of only three *chikan* stitches ever worked in this thread.

Rahet is a stem stitch worked with six threads on the wrong side of the fabric. Working from the left across about four threads, the needle is reinserted halfway along the first stitch, and subsequently where each previous stitch ended. It forms a solid line of back stitch on the right side of the fabric and is rarely used in its simple form but is common in the double form of *dohra bakhya* as an outlining stitch.

Banarsi is a twisted stitch worked with six threads on the right side of the fabric. Working from the right across about five threads, a small stitch is taken over about two threads vertically. The needle is reinserted halfway along and below the horizontal stitch formed and is taken out about two threads vertically on the right above the previous stitch.

Banarsi is a common stitch, used as a decorative outline to a motif, especially in conjunction with *pashni, dohra bakhya, balda* and *zanzeera*. Worked in a circle, it is also part of many combination stitches.

28. *Tepchi pechni.*

29. *Pashni.*

30. *Cutting.*

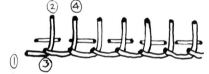

31. *Balda.*

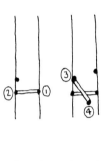

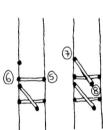

27. *Banarsi.*

Derivatives

These are five in number, four based on *tepchi* and one on *rahet*. They are known as *tepchi pechni, pashni, cutting* or *cutwork, balda* and *dohra bakhya*.

Tepchi pechni. On a basis of *tepchi* forming a stem, and after the flower or design at the end has been worked, the thread is whipped back under the existing stitches, picking up the fabric at approximately every other stitch. It is worked with six threads on the right side of the fabric.

Usually erroneously described as stem stitch, *tepchi pechni* is one of the major stitches of *chikan,* allowing progress along a design without continually finishing off threads. It is the basis of the trailing stems which are such a feature of this embroidery.

Pashni is a fine version of *tepchi pechni* worked with one thread on the right side of the fabric. A row of short running stitches is made on the edge of a motif and the thread is then looped back through them but without picking up the fabric. This forms a laced running stitch. *Pashni* is used as a fine finish on the inside of a motif, as *zanzeera* is on the outside, after the normal outline stitches have been worked. It is not common.

Cutting or cutwork. For this stitch *tepchi* is worked along the inside of scallop shapes and covered with a blanket stitch worked in six threads on the right side of the fabric. It is used for the characteristic scalloped edges of *chikan.* Scallops are occasionally used within a design and always for the edging of an article such as a mat or cloth. Clothing is normally finished with a hem, though the centre back edges of Indo-European infants' robes imitating Ayrshire are usually finished with *cutting.*

Balda. *Tepchi* is worked to outline a motif and is then covered with small vertical satin stitches worked over about two threads from the left. They are pulled tight and rubbed with the thumb to ensure that they are close. *Balda* is worked with six threads on the right side of the fabric. It is used to outline motifs, especially combined with *dohra bakhya, banarsi* and *zanzeera.*

Dohra bakhya. A double row of *rahet* is worked very close together with six threads on the wrong side of the fabric. This gives a double back-stitch effect on the right side, hence the name (*dohra* means double). *Bakhya,* though worked as a close herringbone on the wrong side of the fabric, gives a back stitch on the right side.

Dohra bakhya is used to outline motifs inside *balda* or *banarsi.* It is a very important stitch of *chikan* and is the one most frequently worked in yellow *muga* silk. A design was often marketed in alternative versions, one the normal white *chikan* and the other with all the *dohra bakhya* accentuated in *muga* silk.

32. *Dohra bakhya.*

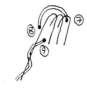

33. *Phunda.*

Murri work

A major feature of *chikan* is the use of a specific formation of stitchery which in itself creates a small embossed leaf or petal. There are seven such stitch formations. They are known as *phunda, mundi murri, nukili murri, mur mora, kauri, boot patti* and *chikan ki ghans*. *Murri* work is often used as a general term to describe these stitches.

Phunda is used to form a small knot-like petal. A blanket stitch is made with a long left arm and two small ones are worked close to it on the right. The needle is then taken around the three stitches to the left side of the first stitch. The long base of the first stitch is then whipped. *Phunda* is worked with six threads on the right side of the fabric. This is one of the best known stitches of *chikan* and is usually wrongly described as a French knot.

Mundi murri is used to form petals with a broad straight edge, tapering to the stem. *Tepchi* is worked from right to left and at the left end is oversewn with two or three straight stitches, keeping the thread to the left with the thumb, and then one or two narrower ones. It is worked with six threads on the right side of the fabric.

Nukili murri is used to form petals tapering at each end. The needle is inserted diagonally across the centre width of the petal

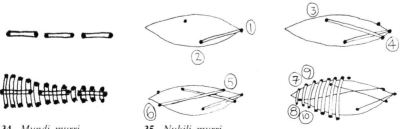

34. *Mundi murri.*　　　**35.** *Nukili murri.*

shape. Then a similar diagonal stitch is taken back towards the base of the petal, and a final narrow diagonal stitch is made across the tip. This forms a thick criss-cross basis which is then oversewn, narrowing at both ends. It is worked with nine threads on the right side of the fabric.

Nukili is the third stitch occasionally worked in *muga* silk, usually when it forms the principal stitch of the whole design.

Phunda, mundi murri and *nukili murri* are the main chunky embossed petal and leaf shapes so characteristic of *chikan*. Of the three *nukili* is the heaviest. When used to form a group of three to five petals rather than individual ones, each of these stitches has *ki patti* added to its name.

Mur mora is used to form a small bud at the end of a curved stem. The shape of a 6 is made with *tepchi* and at the centre the stitch is twisted and overstitched twice. It is worked with six threads on the right side of the fabric.

Kauri is used to form a leaf in the shape of a cowrie shell. Two stitches are worked to three-quarters of the length of the leaf side and the thread is then looped back under the first stitch from the inside without picking up the fabric. It is then taken back through the stitch so formed, finishing with a small stitch at the tip of the leaf. This makes a base down one side of the leaf which is thicker in the centre and which is oversewn with small straight stitches. The work is repeated down the other side of the leaf. It is worked with twelve threads on the right side of the fabric.

Boot patti is used to form a pointed spined leaf. Three large stitches are worked up the spine of the leaf to beyond its tip. The needle is brought out by the side of the point and is reinserted near the centre. Criss-cross stitches are made, picking up the fabric down the spine and keeping very close together on the outside edge. The stitches slant steeply on the right side of the fabric and are straight across the back. *Boot patti* resembles the European open fishbone stitch and is worked with four threads on the right side of the fabric.

Chikan ki ghans is used to form a spiky end to a curved leaf or cone shape, the word *ghans* meaning grass. Staggered long diagonal stitches are worked to a centre line with the thread whipped under them and pulled tight. It is worked with six threads on the right side of the fabric.

Pulled work

The pulled-work stitches of *chikan* are known as *jali*. They are all worked from the back of the fabric with a fine strong thread

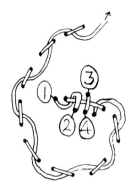

36. *Mur mora.*

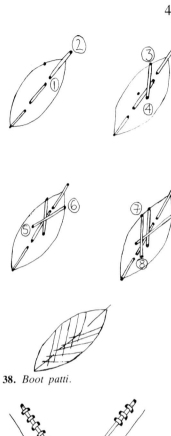

38. *Boot patti.*

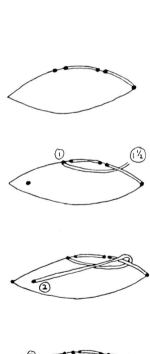

37. *Kauri.*

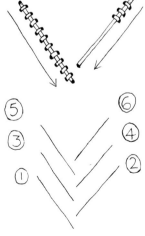

39. *Chikan ki ghans.*

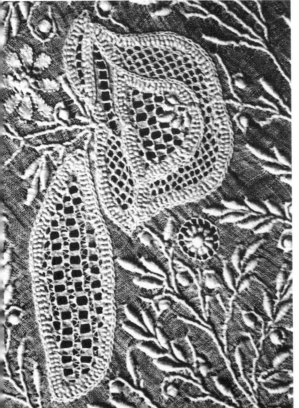

40. This detail shows the following stitches: most outlining in *dohra bakhya* and *zanzeera*; leaves in *chataya*; wings in *hatkati*; stems in *tepchi pechni*; petals mainly in *mundi murri*; some *nukili*, some *kauri* leaves; *mur mora* at the end of stems; some *phunda balda* outlining one motif; some petals in *bakhya*. (Author's collection.)

41. This detail shows the following stitches: outlining in *dohra bakhya* and *zanaeera*; pulled work in a version of *madrasi jali*, also *bangla jali*, *siddhaur jali* and *hatkati*; leaves mainly *nukili* and *phunda bakhya*; small circular flower in a combination of *phunda* encircled with *mundi murri* and *hatkati*. (Courtesy of Joss Graham.)

able to withstand tension. This is usually drawn from the selvedge of the fabric.

Four of the stitches are used to fill leaf or flower shapes. The most common is *siddhaur jali,* which is worked diagonally over six threads, giving small oval holes on the front surface. A variation is *chataya jali,* worked vertically over eight threads and horizontally over four, resulting in a small squared grid.

Bangla jali alternates squares of fabric with square holes and is worked diagonally over fourteen threads. A complicated variation of this, *madrasi jali,* results in a small cross of thread in each of the holes. Unlike a similar stitch in European whitework, the cross is of sewing thread and is not the thread of the fabric left in place.

The common stitch known as *hatkati* is a straight row of pulled holes worked vertically over six to eight threads and is used for the spine of leaves, to encircle flower heads or to divide and edge areas of fabric. Variations of it are *dohra hatkati,* when a double line is made by repeating the stitch on return, and *maheen hatkati,* when it is finely worked over four threads.

42. *Bakhya* is often the predominant stitch of a design, contrasted with touches of pulled work, in this case *chataya* in the large leaf, *hatkati* surrounding the *phunda,* and *murri* forming the flower centres and dotted around the petals. These motifs are then outlined with *dohra bakhya* and *zanzeera. Hatkati* also forms some leaf spines and edges the embroidered area. (Courtesy of Joss Graham.)

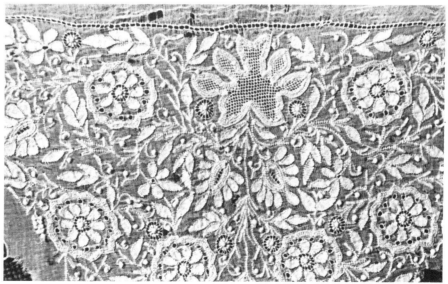

Some variation exists in the spelling of stitch names, particularly *tepchi* (*taipchi*), *murri* (*murree*), *bakhya* (*bukhya*), *phunda* (*phanda*), but the spellings given are those currently used in Lucknow by those involved with *chikan* who are literate.

Appliqué

A rare and very difficult technique of *chikan* is the appliqué work known as *khatao*. Two pieces of fine cotton are superimposed and the edges of the minute design are held by tiny hem stitches. The top layer is then cut away, leaving the pattern in double fabric. This is used as the sole technique in some work or, when combined with stitchery, for seams.

43. *Khatao* is here combined with *hool* and *hat-kati* but more often it is used alone. (Author's collection.)

7
Artisans

The organisation of *chikan* embroidery as a trade is very precise and is controlled by traders (*dookandars*) who are almost without exception Hindu. The other artisans involved are woodblock carvers (*thappagars*), dyers (*rangsaz*), printers (*cheepis*), tailors (*darzis*), embroiderers (*sozankars*) and washermen (*dhobis*). All these trades are passed from father to son or mother to daughter and, apart from *dhobi,* all the names are Persian.

Woodblock carvers

The designs of *chikan* are transferred to the fabric by means of carved woodblocks. These designs belong to the Mughal tradition of decorative arts: tiny petals, floral sprays and tendrils contrasted with a dominant flower head or leaf. The choice of each particular design rests with the woodblock carver. His skill and that of the embroiderer are interdependent: a master embroiderer needs a finely carved pattern to work, a master carver needs a

44. The woodblock designs give some scope to the embroiderer but usually distinguish clearly the areas to be worked in pulled threads. (Photograph: R. Simpson.)

45. Designs from the early twentieth century and the 1980s. The intricacy of the earlier carving would be beyond the skill of most modern embroiderers. (Collection of Kedar Nath Ram Nath, Lucknow.)

skilled embroiderer to execute his design. The deterioration of both these trades has gone hand in hand.

The woodblocks are made from sal wood (*sheesham: Delbergia sisso*), a very hard wood used for doors. Though difficult to carve, it is chosen for its durability. Sal forests predominate in the Dacca area and in the northern parts of the province of Uttar Pradesh, some 50 km (30 miles) from Lucknow.

The carver buys scrap pieces and starts by cutting out the rough shape of the block, which he then paints with thin white emulsion. On this he draws the design freehand with a pencil. He then cuts out the areas between the pattern, using small iron bars flattened at the end like a screwdriver blade, which he hammers with a heavy bar of wood. The bars, known as 'iron pencils' (*kalam*), vary in size. When he has finished, the pattern edges are left raised and, to prevent them eroding, the whole block is dipped in oil.

The carver sells his blocks to the traders and the printers and is independent of the production chain.

Traders

The trader is the kingpin of the *chikan* industry. Most have retail outlets in Lucknow, mainly stalls in the market, and also sell to other parts of India and export via Delhi and Bombay. Every trader employs tailors, printers, embroiderers and washermen, paying them piece rates which he controls entirely. Each of these artisans plays a significant role, the washerman being perhaps the most important, and the embroiderer the lowest paid in the hierarchy.

The trader first decides what is to be made and, if it is an untailored article such as a tablecloth or *sari*, he will cut it

46. The woodblock carver works sitting on the floor of his small open-fronted shop with a large stone as a workbench.

47. Tools for carving blocks. An appropriate size of blade is chosen to gouge out the wood between the pattern lines.

48. Sitting cross-legged on the floor of the printing shop, the dyer stirs the emulsion.

49. The trader selects a design for the printer.

himself. If it is a garment such as a *kurtha* he will pass it to his tailors to cut and stitch. From there it goes to the printer.

Printers

The printer's job is to transfer the design on to the cloth with the carved wooden blocks owned by himself or the trader. The dye he uses is made from the gum which weeps from various varieties of gum trees and which is dried into small lumps. The best quality is from the babul tree (*Acacia arabica*) and looks like clear amber. A darker and more opaque gum is from the dhak tree (*Butea monosperma*).

Pieces of gum are boiled in water and, while they are boiling, powder dye is added to form an emulsion. These dyes are purchased from Delhi, Ahmedabad and Bombay, *indigo jol* being the best quality and *rapid fast* inferior. Magenta colour is chosen for *chikan* as it is easy to see on white. Unlike dyes for print fabrics, no fixative is used, so the dye will wash out.

A cloth pad in a flat tin is saturated with the dye. The fabric to be printed is placed on a surface which must be soft. The wood-block is pressed into the dye tray and then on to the fabric, using a rolling motion. Because of this rolling technique *chikan* blocks have no handle, unlike those for printed fabrics which are not subsequently embroidered.

For a reverse pattern each side of a neck opening, for example, a block of half the pattern is used. It is printed first on one side on the front of the cloth, and then on the other side on the reverse. As the fabric is transparent it is immaterial whether the design is printed on the back or front.

The printer sits at his stall in the market and prints for individuals as well as traders.

Embroiderers

After the printer the trader hands the work to the embroiderers, who are mainly Muslim women, though men and children also help. The women observe *purdah* and all work at home.

First the shadow *bakhya* work is done by one person. If it is a superior piece of *chikan* with embossed *murri* work, this will be done next by a different worker. Finally a third worker adds pulled embroidery. Three to five hours' work a day is all that the embroiderers' eyes will stand.

The embroiderers are paid abysmally and the extent of their poverty is the subject of international concern.

50. Young Muslim girls are being trained as part of a Lucknow scheme to raise the standards of *chikan*.

Masters

However beautiful and skilled, the work of artisans, as opposed to artists, is almost always anonymous. The names of the master embroiderers who worked without financial constraint for the Nawabs are not known; the run-of-the-mill *chikan* of modern times is not worth signing. There are, however, embroiderers working today who have been granted government awards and whose work is commissioned. Most are the sons and daughters of the last two great masters of Lucknow, Faiyaz Khan and Hasan Mirsa, both of whom died in the early 1980s.

Faiyaz Khan began to embroider at the age of six and by his sixties was blind and destitute. He was a law unto himself and though he never strayed from the classic repertoire of stitches, he was immensely inventive in the variety he used. He drew many of his designs himself, incorporating the small elephants, deer, peacocks and tigers that decorated the animal trappings made by the goldwork embroiderers of Lucknow, and the fish that was the emblem of the Nawabs.

His embroidery features an outline stitch that no one else uses. It is called *dhum* and consists of two parallel lines of *tepchi* with *cutting* worked over each, giving a fairly wide line with a ridged spine.

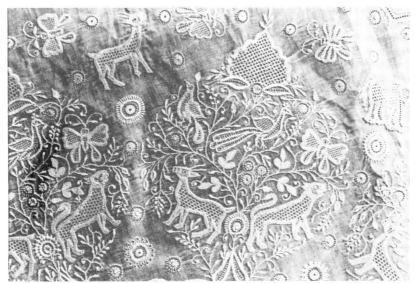

51. Though the master
Faiyaz Khan kept strictly to
the traditional stitches of *chikan*, his work was inventive,
delicately balanced and very
personal. (Central Design
Centre, Lucknow.)

52. The stitchery on this
anokhi handkerchief of
Hasan Mirsa pierces only
half the depth of the fabric
and is barely visible on the
back — a *tour de force* of
incredible skill. (Central Design Centre, Lucknow.)

53. All day long washermen scrub hundreds of newly finished *chikan kurthas* and cloths in the Gomti river at Lucknow.

Even the delicacy of Faiyaz Khan's work is surpassed by one particular technique of Hasan Mirsa's that he called *anokhi*. On diaphanous cotton of some 38 threads to the centimetre, he embroidered by splitting the threads across their depth so that the stitchery did not penetrate to the back of the fabric. Such skill defies belief.

Both these masters worked to commission and sold their embroideries through government emporia. Helped by their

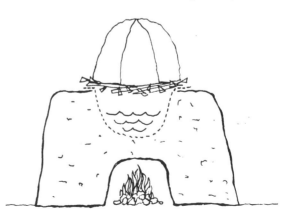

54. *Bhatt* for removing the dye from *chikan* embroideries, which are piled on top of the sticks, covered with a plastic cloth and left to steam all night.

55. A simple washbowl is made by lining a hole on the river bank with plastic.
56. The final scrub and pounding.

families, they also worked for the traders. Examples of their embroideries are in the Crafts Museum at the Central Design Centre in Lucknow.

Washermen

The Gomti river, which flows through Lucknow, passes the banks of *Sheishmahal,* the hall of mirrors, to the north of the town. Here the washermen work and lines and lines of clean *chikan* embroideries, strictly divided by colour — turquoise in one batch, shades of beige, pinks, corals and reds, peacock blues and parrot greens, amid masses and masses of whites — flap in the sunshine. Up to their knees in the river, thirty to forty washermen can be seen every day standing by their ridged washboards, raising a *kurtha* or tablecloth high in the air and slamming it down on to the board with a resounding thud. But this is only the public part of their work.

When the washerman first receives the embroideries from the

trader, so many filthy crumpled rags stained with magenta, he dips each in a bowl of soapy water and piles them on the ground of his backyard. Here he has a clay oven (*bhatt*). This is a square construction about a metre (39 inches) high with a hollow in the middle containing a deep bowl of water, below which a fire is lit. The top of the bowl is criss-crossed with sticks and on these the washerman places a pile of the soaked embroideries. He then covers it with a plastic cloth and leaves it to steam all night. This removes the magenta dye.

The next stage is done by the river or, if the washerman lives in an outlying village, in the local pond or stream. Large holes dug along the banks are lined with plastic and filled with soapy water in which the embroideries are washed, sorted by colour. The soap is a dry acidic salt (*rehu*) extracted from the earth and in appearance like white sand. Then follows the spectacular pounding on the washboards in the river.

A starch is prepared by boiling rice in water and skimming off the lather. This lather is mixed with water to form a rice paste (*peech*), into which the embroideries are dipped then hung on the lines to dry. White embroideries are also dipped into bowls of blue bleach (*neel*).

Finally, the washermen's womenfolk iron the embroideries with large heavy irons filled with glowing coals. The embroideries remain grouped by colour throughout all the processes.

57. The washermen's wives use heavy irons filled with glowing coals for the final process in the preparation of *chikan*.

8
The present situation

Bengal

The partition of India in 1947 split Bengal in two, leaving Calcutta the capital of the state of West Bengal in India, and Dacca (now written Dhaka) the capital of East Pakistan, independent since 1971 under the name of Bangladesh. Dacca still has the air of a provincial rather than a national capital, its streets flanked by parks and thronged with brightly painted rickshaws. The urban horror of Calcutta, with its millions living on pavements and in shacks, is tempered by the palatial Doric columns and grandiose facades of the buildings of the British Raj. They are very different cities.

Today there is no trace of *chikan* in either city and nothing in their museum collections save some pieces from Lucknow in the Indian Museum of Calcutta. The textile heritage of Dacca is considered to reside in muslins, in *jamdani* weavings and in the quilts known as *kanthas* made by women for their own use. The only whitework is modern silk gauze tablecloths tamboured with silk floss in simple patterns and also cotton caps for Muslim men embroidered with European-style daisies in shadow stitch. These same daisies are worked in multicoloured shadow stitch on organdie tablecloths in Calcutta. They are referred to as Bengali embroidery and the word *chikan* in both Dacca and Calcutta today draws a blank stare, whereas in Lucknow it is still the major industry.

Lucknow

Lucknow is now a town of seedy grandeur, somewhat off the beaten tourist track. A thousand cusped arches, a hundred cupolas adorn the facades of the sadly neglected royal residences and mosques; magnificent decayed palaces approached by impressive flights of steps are empty inside apart from the odd swinging broken chandelier; a solitary elephant wanders up the dusty street; the old Residency is haunted by ghosts of the besieged English in the Mutiny, a shaft of brilliant sunlight penetrating the dark room in which they were imprisoned, a wall plaque commemorating a nineteen-year-old girl killed by a cannonball. To the visitor Lucknow is an evocative and attractive town.

35 per cent of its 1,300,000 inhabitants are Muslim and most of them are *chikan* workers, though no census of their precise

number exists. They live in the run-down areas of the city, in cramped ghetto-like conditions, and in the villages around, where they have built themselves makeshift homes on public land.

The decline of the *chikan* embroidery of Lucknow has been a gradual, ineluctable process from the days of the wealthy courts of Oudh, through the removal of patronage because of the dwindling power of the Nawabs in the nineteenth century and the end of the feudal *zamdari* system of land ownership, to the emergence of *chikan* as a traded commodity. High-quality goods, requiring hours of fine, skilled work, could not compete in the newer, open-market conditions. The cotton-mill industry of India developed, fashions changed and poor-quality handcrafted goods, not only in textiles, sold easily and in quantity.

From the late 1940s on, various schemes have been devised to improve the quality of *chikan*. These are always instigated by sociologists or sociological organisations with the aim of improving the economic lot of the workers and their families. Though the sociologist rewards the worker slightly more justly and produces a higher quality of work costing more and reviving more of the old stitches, the Hindu trader still dominates the industry.

Hope for the future lies mostly with the young 'government awardees', whose work for museums and knowledgeable patrons preserves the true quality of *chikan,* this unique and eclectic embroidery derived from the cultures of Europe, the Islamic world and India.

9
Places to visit

GREAT BRITAIN
Embroidery on display

Guildford Museum, Castle Arch, Quarry Street, Guildford, Surrey GU1 3SX. Telephone: 0483 503497 extensions 3540/1/2/ 3. General and Anglo-Indian embroidery.

Royal Museum of Scotland, Queen Street, Edinburgh EH2 1JD. Telephone: 031-225 7534. Ayrshire embroidery.

Victoria and Albert Museum, Cromwell Road, South Kensington, London SW7 2RL. Telephone: 01-938 8500. General embroidery, including Indian; Gallery India, 1550-1850.

Indian associations

Bruce Castle Museum, Lordship Lane, Tottenham, London N17 8NU. Telephone: 01-808 8772. Indian room settings.

Knebworth House, Knebworth, Hertfordshire SG3 6PY. Telephone: 0438 812661. The Delhi Durbar.

Powis Castle, Welshpool, Powys SY21 8RF. Telephone: 0938 4336. Clive of India Museum.

58. Ornate palaces and mosques from the period of Nawabi rule give Lucknow an air of decayed grandeur.

INDIA
Chikan embroidery on display
Bharat Kala Bhawan, Benares Hindu University, Varanasi, Uttar Pradesh.

Calico Museum of Textiles, Calico Mills, outside Jamalpur Gate, Ahmedabad 22, Gujarat.

Crafts Museum, Central Design Centre, 8 Cantonment Road, Lucknow, Uttar Pradesh.

Indian Museum, 27 Jawaharlal Nehru Road, Calcutta 13, West Bengal.

State Museum, Banarasibagh, Lucknow, Uttar Pradesh.

10
Further reading

There are no books on *chikan*. Background reading could include the following:

Court life and arts under Mughal rule

Archer, Mildred; Rowell, Christopher; and Skelton, Robert. *Treasures from India: The Clive Collection at Powis Castle*. National Trust, 1987.

Gascoigne, Bamber. *The Great Moghals*. Jonathan Cape, 1987.

Patnaik, Naveen. *A Second Paradise: Indian Courtly Life*. Sidgwick and Jackson, 1985.

Sharar, Abul Halim. *Lucknow: The Last Phase of an Oriental Culture*. UNESCO translation by E. S. Harcourt and F. Hussain. Paul Elek, 1975.

Skelton, Robert. *The Indian Heritage: Court Life and Arts under Mughal Rule*. Victoria and Albert Museum, 1982.

Letters and memoirs of Englishwomen in India

Dunbar, Janet. *Tigers, Durbars and Kings: Fanny Eden's Indian Journals 1837-1838*. John Murray, 1988.

Fay, Mrs Eliza. *Original Letters from India (1779-1815)*. The Hogarth Press, 1986.

Macmillan, Margaret. *Women of the Raj*. Thames and Hudson, 1988.

Pemble, John (editor). *Miss Fane in India*. Alan Sutton, Gloucester, 1985.

Sattin, Anthony (editor). *An Englishwoman in India: The Memoirs of Harriet Tytler 1828-1858*. Oxford University Press, 1988.

Wilson, Lady. *Letters from India*. Century, 1984.

Embroidery

Stockley, Beth. *Woven Air*. Whitechapel Art Gallery, 1988. Bengali embroidery and *jamdani*.

Swain, Margaret. *Ayrshire and Other Whitework*. Shire, 1982.

60

Index

Page numbers in italic refer to illustrations